FLOWER CHILD

Janrose Kasmir

Copyright © 2017 Janrose Kasmir

All rights reserved.

ISBN: 978-1982048884

DEDICATION

At the center of my universe, resides the best thing that ever happened to me, my daughter Lisa Ann Kasmir. I never cease to be amazed by how talented, smart, and thoughtful you are. I will take credit for making you, but you deserve all the credit for making you into who you are now.

And to Dizzy Gillespie, my good friend. Before he passed, I promised him that when I wrote a book, I would dedicate it to him. So, here it is, Dizzy, as promised. Peace.

CONTENTS

	Acknowledgments	vii
1	The Beginning	1
2	The History	8
3	The Moment of the Photograph	18
4	Our Shared Future	23

Janrose Kasmir

ACKNOWLEDGMENTS

I want to thank Catherine Riboud for her generous permission to use Marc Riboud's photos. I also want thank Bonnie Hill Hearn for all her help in birthing this book and Adam Karpinski for his cover and book design. This book is the story of what happened the day of the photo, and I hope it, in some small part, furthers my quest for peace.

I want to also extend my thanks to Ken Scott for his help with shaping my autobiography. His work was greatly appreciated.

Most of all, I want to thank Marc Riboud for helping me believe in myself as a peace pilgrim. His kind words inspired me, and his photos affirm my role as a peacemaker every day of my life.

THE BEGINNING
RIDERS ON THE STORM

The teenage girl in the photograph is holding a flower, a chrysanthemum a hippie chick gave to her at the Anti-War March to the Pentagon in Washington, D.C. Looking at the photo now, what is most remarkable to me is the profound sadness on her face. Her hands are clasped prayerfully as she looks directly at the soldiers. Their eyes are averted, and although their guns are pointing straight at her, she feels no fear.

I know what she saw and how she felt that day because I am that girl.

At the time I heard about the march, I was only seventeen, and I felt as if my life was over. I could not have been more miserable. I slept up to ten hours a day at my foster home. But then I heard about the demonstration that was taking place in Washington to protest the war in Vietnam, and suddenly I had a purpose. Finally, something was worth staying awake for.

I had been reading accounts about the war in the *Washington Post* and speaking with my friends. Everything I read confirmed my belief that we had no business imposing our will onto another country's civil war. I had absolutely no trust in the Establishment and knew that all the bullshite they were feeding the public about the domino theory, (that is, if Vietnam fell to communism, then all of Southeast Asia would fall) could not be trusted. We were being manipulated with "boogie man" politics. The government was counting on the fact that one cannot be afraid and think at the same time; consequently, we were easily manipulated into believing anything the government wanted us to believe. The hippies claimed the basic truth of politics was, "If you sell them fear, you can sell them anything." (I pray these lessons are not lost on us now.)

Straight people never seemed to stop and question the other possible reasons for being in Vietnam, like the CIA using Air America to ship out heroin for profit, or the fact that war is big business. Most of the American public just seemed to hold onto whatever they were told, believing whatever the government said was gospel. But not I! I wanted the truth, and still do to this day. I have never confirmed what the whole truth of that war was.

FLOWER CHILD

I was living with a foster family because of a legal hassle I will explain shortly. For now, suffice it to say that my foster parents acted with the authority of my parents, and their word was law. I was uncertain how they would feel about my going to the demonstration. I understood that my foster mother, Madame Sagan, was a true martyr for peace. She worked for the Resistance D'Italian during World War II, and although she shared with me that she had been captured and tortured by the Nazis, she never went into many details. All I knew was that her wrists were crushed, a bullet grazed her neck, and if the war had lasted longer, she would not have survived. Many years later, I heard her heroic tale—that while she was held by the Nazis, a defector slipped a note to her in a piece of bread with the word "courage" the night before she was to be shot. Instead, she was rescued. Her heroics during the war included releasing prisoners from trains and smuggling radio equipment across Nazi lines. She received a special Medal of Honor, one of seven awarded by Italian government for her bravery.

She founded the North American Chapter of Amnesty International, and while I was with her, I helped Amnesty fight the Greek junta. It was only a small effort, but I helped reveal the identity of a person trying to propagandize the Junta with a letter to the editor in the *Washington Post*. I identified the individual as a foreign agent instead of the private citizen that person was pretending to be. I was praised and thanked for my work by Amnesty International and my foster mother, which meant a great deal to me.

The morning of the demonstration, I was elated and clueless. I'd never been to a demonstration before, so I really didn't know what to expect, but I was excited at the prospect of meeting other hippies like me. It was rumored that the demonstrators could number fifty thousand. Later, I would learn that the march was estimated at more than one hundred thousand participants. The Yippies were going to be there flying their flag, the marijuana leaf. They could always be counted on to have good dope. I couldn't wait to see the Yippies and in particular Abbie Hoffman and Jerry Rubin, who were the most famous members of the group. The Yippies appeared frequently at anti-war demonstrations with dozens of their flags. It had a black background with a five-pointed red star in the center and a green cannabis leaf superimposed over it. Once, when asked about the Yippie flag, an anonymous Yippie told the *New York Times,* "The black is for anarchy, the red star is for our five-point program, and the leaf is for marijuana, which is how we get ecologically stoned without polluting the environment." I loved that story. Mostly, I loved their sense of humor, pranks, and their belief that we were here to change the world for the better.

I hadn't said anything to the Sagans about wanting to go to the demonstration. I knew they believed in the peace cause, so I didn't think they would stop me, but I really didn't want them interfering or getting worried, so I planned my escape for right after breakfast, when I knew everyone would be too busy to notice me slipping out the door. Even though we had our good moments, I still did not trust that Madame and her husband would allow me to go to the demonstration, and I knew I must go no matter what!

I quietly readied myself, choosing a special outfit in case I met a guy like me, a hippie who cared about peace and love. Especially love. I decided on my pink crepe paisley shift, as it seemed to be the most slimming outfit I owned. The last thing I wanted was to look fat, and I was afraid I might. Still, I had to push through the constant dread I felt whenever I ventured out into the world. I hated my looks. I was too tall, overweight, and I always had pimples that reliably blossomed on any social occasion. True to form, I was broken out for the march.

I put on my watch with the hand-stamped leather band I had tooled. Hand crafts were my passion, and I loved to show them off. My mother was an art teacher, and I grew up having all kinds of materials in the basement that I could play with. We had a potters wheel, a copper enameling kiln, and many different tools for all kinds of art projects. There were papers of every description for origami or drawing—although drawing was a problem. Ever since my mother had two paraplegic students who out-drew me using chunks of chalk between their toes, I was too embarrassed to try it anymore.

I was afraid to wear makeup to the march because inevitably the mascara would run and leave me looking like a raccoon with black circles under my eyes, so I decided that I would pass on it. With that final decision out of the way, I was ready to leave. I put on my tall brown leather boots and then took a final look at myself in the mirror. At least my hair, which I had just recently cut myself, pleased me.

I had only a few dollars on me, but that would be enough for bus fare to and from downtown Washington. I just had to get as far as the Washington Monument grounds on Constitution Avenue and 17th Street. I was living in Rockville, so I would have to travel to the main bus terminal on the Maryland, Washington, DC border first and then transfer. No big deal, I thought. I had gotten around Washington by bus before.

Quietly I stepped slowly toward the door, dreading the thought that anyone would see me. It was early on Saturday, and as usual, the Sagans seemed to have something that was keeping them busy, just as I had anticipated. I got to the door without spotting anyone, and in a moment, I was out of there and free!

I broke into a run and kept it up for a few blocks until I felt safe. I had to stop to catch my breath. Even though I did a ton of sports when I was in elementary school, I had not kept it up, so I was easily winded.

"Free at last! free at last! Thank God almighty I am free at last"

Whenever I felt I had escaped danger, Reverend King's words always came to me.

I was just really glad that I escaped the house without getting busted. With only a few more blocks to walk to the bus stop, I looked around, hoping I might see some of my friends. When I had asked around if they were going to the demonstration, almost everyone had a lame excuse. I couldn't tell if they weren't going or if they were trying to ditch me. That's when I decided to go on my own.

Even though I had taken a bus downtown many times, this was something special and exciting, and I felt as if I were looking at old sights with new eyes. Even the familiar appeared different. The trees were still flushed with fall colors, painting the streets in magical hues. As I got closer to downtown and gazed out the window, I noticed that the normally quiet downtown shopping vista had started changing. The usual Saturday afternoon crowds of shoppers were replaced by middle-aged, middle-class people walking in small clusters. Some people carried signs; some were holding hands. Mommies pushed baby strollers. Priests and nuns in small groups walked solemnly. Everybody seemed to be heading to the same place.

Because I arrived late, I didn't hear any speeches. People seemed to be marching toward the 14th Street Bridge and the Pentagon, so I fell in step. I saw a group of mostly young men who were carrying a banner that read "Youth Against Fascism." I didn't feel I could argue with that sentiment, so I joined them. (A week later, I attended a meeting of this group and sadly realized they were an anti-Zion organization, mostly made up of Palestinians. I stayed at the meeting long enough to hear them praising the murder of Jews. That was my signal to get out if there!)

As we marched, they shouted, "Viva Ché!" I had no idea what a Ché was but did my best to join in with the shouting. The immediate sense of camaraderie made me feel as if I were part of something important. We all knew why we were here. We were working together to stop the war machine. I was so moved by the presence of so many people, that I fell to my knees, and started singing "God Bless America."

Once on my feet again, I proceeded to walk with the flow of the crowd. A hippie chick was handing out flowers to anyone who would take them—bright chrysanthemums as bright as the day and the hope in my heart. I reached out my hand and gratefully took the flower from her. I clutched it tightly and continued to walk, marching in time with the crowd.

THE HISTORY
PEOPLE ARE STRANGE

*T**he girl in the photo is holding a flower and longing for peace.*

As I marched forward, making my way to the Pentagon, the din of noise engulfed me and kept me focused in the moment. The shouting from the crowd was a rallying cry for peace, and yet the air was charged with a fighting spirit. This was not like the humble dignified marches I heard about in the civil rights movement in places like Selma, Alabama. Dr. King was so careful to be sure nobody gave The Man an excuse to beat their heads in, as if The Man needed an excuse. King was careful not to antagonize the police, lose dignity, or betray his cause. Even so, his people were brutally beaten with nightsticks, sprayed with fire hoses, and attacked by police dogs. This march was different.

Clearly, the police and soldiers stonewalled us, averting their eyes, never looking directly at us, as if to say we did not matter. If necessary, I would sacrifice myself to this cause that was so much more important than me and my life. I would die for my cause if I must, although, in reality, I felt no threat of harm. In fact, the police and National Guard seemed to be trying to protect us from ourselves.

We were angry, and we were tired of the Establishment lying to us and ripping us off. We were tired of our young people being blown to pieces in foreign lands for something that was so wrong. Vietnam was in the throes of a civil war in which we had no right to be involved.

I wanted my life to make a difference, and I cared about my brothers and sisters who were dying in Vietnam, regardless of whether they were Vietcong or Vietnamese. These people were dying for what? So some CIA bastards could make money shipping heroin? I believed what I heard about Air America being a covert operation by the CIA to ship heroin, and I absolutely believed that people in government were getting rich off the blood of our poor soldiers and the Vietnamese people. It disgusted me to my core.

Later I would learn that the CIA enabled drug dealing as a tactic for obtaining money for a variety of purposes. This included funding the Contras. It seems that the CIA helped them by paving the way for the sale of illicit drugs in America, thus funding the operations of the Contras. The CIA is a dangerous, rogue operation that operates outside the law and though their power is well beyond my ability to limit, I will always speak out on their foul, illegal, and immoral business.

We believed that all the talk our government was spouting about the Domino Effect and communism was a lie with a purpose. The establishment wanted us to believe that all Southeast Asia would fall to communism after Vietnam fell, toppling like domino tiles. This was the government's attempt to justify its wars in Vietnam, Laos, and Cambodia. I could not and would not disconnect myself from my feelings for the plight of the people in Vietnam. I felt very strongly that we were all part of the human race! I believed there was no separation between people, that we were all more alike than we were different. Even though these were a people that looked very different from us, people who lived a half a world away, I felt no distance between us. These men and women, young and old humans of flesh and blood were as entitled to life as any of my neighbors or family. We were all in this life and this world together.

I fondly remembered a book my mother gave me when I was very young, probably six or seven years old. It was called *The Family of Man*, and it contained pictures of people from all over the world, grouped into families bearing obvious similarities. On the cover, an Asian man in a big floppy hat played a wooden flute, while someone who looked like him stood behind him, smiling. It was a sweet image that invited me to care about these people I saw in a very personal way. I never realized what an impact the book had on me until I found myself repeating the phrase, "the family of man," throughout my life.

How did I become so committed to peace and right that I was willing to die for a cause? Certainly, Dr. King inspired me with his elegant speeches, his total commitment to non-violence, his reverence for the ways of Gandhi, and his dignity and religious adherence to the principles of goodness. He inspired me to strive for higher consciousness and better behavior. Dr. King made me want to be a better person.

I was passionately angry about the Establishment's lies that got us into the war. I felt that Amerika, as we called it, was trying to kill my brothers and sisters in a faraway land, and that my government had no right to use its military might against a small sovereign nation.

The inhumanity of America's position disgusted me and motivated me to come out and protest. But how did I get to be so concerned about the underdog? How did I care so passionately about people so many thousands of miles away?

The first unintended assault to my humanity came with my sister's death when I was twelve. Losing her emotionally devastated me. What destroyed me was the dissolution of my family. Just as I was entering puberty, my world fell apart. My parents became depressed and removed, and I was pretty much left to my own devices. While it is true that I could have tried to strike back at the world for destroying my family, somehow, instead, I went the other direction and became sensitized and deeply concerned about the needs of others.

I had a strong need to feel worthy, and the only way I could justify my existence was to be of use to others, so from a very early age I was passionate about caring for other people. I loved being helpful.

At the age of fifteen, I formalized my helping by volunteering for the Red Cross at a nursing home. I wanted to be useful, but most of all, I wanted to be appreciated. At the age of twenty-eight, I received the gift of sobriety. After years of horrible experiences with drug and alcohol abuse, I knew that if I did not clean up, I would die. There were many false starts and failures, but finally I began to recover, and I felt compelled to return that miraculous gift by starting and maintaining spiritual fellowship groups in prisons and institutions for both adult and juvenile facilities. I was taught that I could only keep my gift by giving it away, so I faithfully continued doing service for about ten years. Ultimately, I always received more than I gave.

I always craved feeling that I was worth something to someone. Throughout my life, I looked for external sources of validation. The right guy, good grades, Girl Scout honor badges, or whatever else affirmed my sense that I was a worthwhile, valuable human being. I believe that I was very lucky that the hippie movement came along the way it did because I embraced those values to create my identity.

It was a funny twist of logic that held us hippies together. We were nonconformists conforming to a code of behavior. We were non-joiners, outcasts who clung to our fellow outcasts. We believed in truth and right. I am not sure how we got so smart, but we cared about our environment and our fellow beings. We followed the ways of Gandhi, Lao Tsu and to a lesser degree, Confucius. We embraced Carlos Castaneda as a great shaman and tried to emulate his psychedelic journeys. Though many of us skeptically listened to Timothy Leary, mostly we conceded to some of his advice and dropped acid in an attempt to tune in, turn on, and drop out. Dr. King was our hero. We also admired farm worker leader Cesar Chavez for his sheer fortitude, guts, and his dedication to improving the lives of oppressed migrant farm workers. We were inspired by the good word and works of our heroes and vowed to follow their example of goodness and strength of character. They motivated us to become better people.

Exactly why the Vietnam War erupted as the focal point of our protests is hard to say, but I knew in my heart of hearts, that I would take a stand for peace with my dying breath.

The division within our society was the "Us's" against the "Thems," the Establishment. We could easily identify like-minded people in the beginning by the guys wearing long hair. It was wonderful in the early days to be able to trust someone by virtue of the length of their locks. That signal broke down because long hair became popular, and we had to become more cautious. The entire hippie scene was a phenomenon, not unlike the Old West. It was a happening complete with uniforms, a language of our own, and a well-defined belief system that began with an innocent belief in sex, drugs, and rock 'n' roll—all of which were meant to bring us closer together.

I understood why Buffalo Bill wanted to preserve the Old West with the creation of his Wild West Show. He knew this was a time in our history that would disappear shortly and be erased from existence forever. Unfortunately, we hippies did not have the foresight to preserve our culture, which was pronounced dead at the Funeral for the Flowerchild held in San Francisco in the 1960s. However, we see vestiges of our hippie traditions around the world in places like Christiania in Denmark.

In our heyday, we had a great look and a wonderful credo. We believed that love conquered all. In our world, good won out over evil. There were paranoid moments when we worried about the FBI tapping our phones and trying to bust us for pot, but generally we stayed high in thought and deed.

That day at the march, I wondered if my foster parents were wondering where I was. Perhaps they didn't even miss me. Maybe they were happy I wasn't around. I didn't think I brought them much happiness. I believed they were trying to help, but understandably that gets old at some point if there is no real love in return. Suddenly the big picture exploded in my brain. My foster home was the key to my revelation.

I was placed with the Sagans because I had been locked up for ten months as the result of a bust for marijuana. I attended a crazy group therapy starting when I was fifteen. Crazy is not a big enough word to describe that therapy group. Although it was supposed to provide help for teenagers with unhealthy behaviors, that group was more like a circus than a therapy session. People took turns hurting themselves and acting out other unhealthy behaviors. Almost everyone took turns locking him or herself in a bathroom, smashing coke bottles and threatening to do bodily harm by cutting wrists with broken shards of glass. This was staged regularly: different week, same behavior, different player. The abuse got old and tired, so something new was tried. People got very drunk. That wasn't enough, so people started overdosing on pills, timing their obvious impairment for near the end of group, with plenty of time for an ambulance to come to the rescue.

In the midst of all that mayhem, I made a friend, Mandy (not her real name). I was sixteen and only about one year older than she. We were both students. She lived at home but would run away from time to time.

As a favor to her, I purchased a baggy full of

marijuana for fifteen dollars. The quality was all right, although it was pretty loaded with stems and seeds. It was called an ounce, but I had no idea of the true weight. Still, for the price she paid, it was a good deal. I gave it to her after group one day and didn't think about it again—until months later, my dad got a call from Montgomery County Detective Steve Filyo, his real name, asking my dad to bring me down to the police station immediately.

I had no idea what was happening. We arrived, and my dad was immediately ushered into a room by Sgt. Filyo. I was left in the outer office. The longest ten minutes of my life passed before they returned, whereupon my father hauled off and slammed me across the face with a clenched fist, knocking me across the room. I saw stars.

Filyo quickly pulled me into his office, motioning for my father to wait.

This all took place in 1967 before In re: Gault gave juveniles the same rights as adults in the court system. I ended up facing a kangaroo court, with no rights, and a presiding judge who thought this was *Father Knows Best.*

Filyo encouraged me to incriminate myself. I innocently complied giving away what few rights I had to any defense. Consequently, I cooked my own goose because I was honest and easily manipulated by this soft-spoken, blue-eyed, good-looking detective.

Because of that entrapment, I spent ten months in a state mental hospital. At a time in life when most seventeen-year-olds are developing their identity through loving encouragement and careful guidance, I was terrorized by exposure to grotesque humans at the lowest moments in their lives. I watched self-mutilation become a group sport, as individuals cleverly invented new ways to outwit their protective environment. Staples were pulled out of magazines and swallowed. Other small objects were found and consumed. People bragged about X-rays that were ordered to discover where the foreign objects were lodged in their bodies. On the wards, pills were bought and sold for candy bars, a practice I missed when I returned to the streets. This was my adolescent learning curve.

From the first night I spent there, I awoke precisely at midnight screaming at the top of my lungs, according the nurses' report. Those night terrors have never left. Ultimately, this is what I fought against: the injustice of a system that mentally raped me when I was a teenager as a consequence of breaking this country's drug laws.

The greatest irony was the final words of Alfred D. Noyes*, the presiding judge. After passing sentence, he said, "Don't think of your time there as punitive. Rather think of it as rehabilitative."

Who was he kidding?

Humans are complex beings. Peace is a complex issue. Understanding my dedication to serve peace is not a simple task, but one I understand better as I get older. I care deeply about my brothers and sisters in foreign lands, and my true desire is to protect them from the aggression of American business and political interests. I feel a kinship with them and their anger over being violated by Goliath.

Pure rage boiled my blood and incited me to dedicate myself to fighting the cruel injustice of it all. I hated the Establishment for sacrificing lives on the altar of that horrible war. I hated the Establishment for destroying the psyche of this teenager for a simple indiscretion. I knew what it meant to be a victim of the system, to suffer terribly for the crime of committing an innocent mistake. I take responsibility for bad judgment; however, I do not accept the consequences as just. I grieve for the loss of my healthy adolescent psyche. I take up the fight for the rights of all of those wronged by Amerika.

Looking back in time, I better understand my place at that march and many others. I simply could *NOT* not go. The need to join marches for peace is infused into my heart, my brain and my DNA.

Once at the march, I fell in step with people who were there for like-minded reasons, and those who were not. My message was carried with my body in the hope that I would make a difference. I prayed for peace and marched for the message, "Give peace a chance."

THE MOMENT OF THE PHOTOGRAPH
I GET AROUND

*T**he girl in the photograph is holding a flower, clasped tightly in her hands. She began by praying for the victims of war. Now, her consciousness is changing, distracted by her need to understand what is happening at that moment. She looks directly at the soldiers, although their eyes are averted. She feels invisible, although their guns are pointing straight at her.*

Ironically, at that moment she feels no fear, protected by her seeming lack of existence.

The day was getting late as we made our way together, marching to the beat of an invisible drum. We pushed on together, a huge wave of humanity, more than one hundred thousand people, washing over the 14th Street Bridge, in the heart of Washington, DC, to the center of the war machine, the Pentagon.

I heard that Allen Ginsberg was working to levitate the Pentagon, so occasionally I would look up to see if it was flying by overhead, but no such luck.

As we made our way together, I was struck by how normal everyone looked. Where I lived, I was completely isolated from anyone other than my hippie friends, who were also against the war. I attended a night class to get my high school diploma. While there, I got into a terrible fight with a young woman slightly older than I, whose brother was serving in Vietnam. She told me I was a traitor and a commie lover. I was sure I wasn't a traitor because I felt my beliefs were on the side of right! As for loving communists, I wasn't sure how to respond to that. I didn't think I had ever met a communist, so I had to reserve judgment. Actually, I knew her response was really more about trying to hurt my feelings than to accurately describe my character flaws. Finally, the teacher intervened in what quickly became a shouting match. I called her a war monger and brain dead for standing up for a policy she did not understand. She called me a dirty hippie. Later, I realized that mostly she was terrified about her brother's jeopardy in the midst of that terrible war. It was all so sad and so wrong.

As we started to approach the Pentagon, out of nowhere, a line of National Guardsmen appeared, standing between us and the Puzzle Palace. I honestly had no idea what I would do once I got to the Pentagon, but at that moment, it didn't matter. The immediate problem was dealing with what was in front of my face.

There was a blockade of soldiers that had to be reckoned with.

They were lined up, shoulder to shoulder, with their bayoneted guns pointing straight ahead. I tried to make eye contact with the soldiers, but that wasn't happening. I realized at that moment where the saying, "stonewalled" came from, because that was what I was up against. Their eyes were glazed, and they seemed to be made of stone—certainly not flesh and blood, living, breathing, or thinking. Just a wall of stone.

Immediately, I tried to engage them.

"Come on! Why don't you just throw down your guns and join us? You don't really want to shoot me, do you?"

Nothing.

I spread my arms out, to look like Jesus on the cross.

"Come on. What are you going to do? Do you want to kill me?"

Nothing.

"Come on. Make love not war. Don't you realize we could be having fun instead of this? Throw down your weapons and join us!"

Nothing.

Finally, I shouted, "What are you going to do, shoot me?"

Suddenly, a large bank of floodlights came on, and I wondered if there were TV cameras filming this. However, my distraction was fleeting, and the soldiers once again captured my attention.

FLOWER CHILD

Abruptly, the din of the crowd muted into a soft blur of noise. Something was starting to happen in my psyche. The soldiers I had been shouting at came into a hard focus. I stopped looking at their uniforms and started focusing on their faces. Young faces.

A great sadness came over me. I clutched my flower tightly. A shift in my perception was erupting, shattering the rhetoric that shaped my perception. I stopped looking and started seeing with vision.

Up until that moment, I was fighting the rhetoric: the baby killers, the war machine, the evil that the soldiers represented. Suddenly, the rhetoric melted away, dropping like a veil to reveal the truth of the moment. These were young boys I faced, more innocent than evil—less a symbol and more real humans. They were fresh flesh and blood. Each of these boys could have been my brother, my lover, a childhood playmate. These soldier boys standing before me were just as much victims of the war effort as the people they were fighting.

In that moment the photographer immortalized, the young soldier's uniform melted away, and all I could see was this young being's sweet face. I now saw with clear vision, embracing my former enemy, and all became one. Simpatico.

There was no division between these young boys and me and the people they fought against. We were all victims of war. I saw clearly that we were all the losers. And I was fighting something bigger than all of us, something very evil.

This was all too big for me to grasp at that moment. It was enough for me to be terribly sad for these poor young boys who were led off to fight, to sacrifice their bodies on the altar of some terrible greed we call war.

Right then, I swore I would dedicate my life to finding a peaceful answer to these horrors. I knew what was happening was wrong. I just wasn't sure how to make it right.

OUR SHARED FUTURE
IF I HAD A HAMMER

The girl in the photograph is holding a flower, a chrysanthemum a hippie chick gave to her at the Anti-War March to the Pentagon. Looking at the photo now, what is most remarkable to me is the profound sadness on her face. These soldier boys standing before her were just as much victims of the war effort as the people they were shooting at. They were the puppets of the power that sat safely back in Washington, manipulating these young men with the stroke of a pen, sacrificing their lives for power and greed.

Looking back now, fifty years after that photo was taken, I realize the time has come to dedicate myself fulltime to the struggle for peace and finish the journey I began so many years ago. I have so much more understanding that can serve me as I go forward with my mission. I call it a mission of peace, primarily because when I serve others, I am at peace.

I believe we can all have our material needs met if we realize we have enough and are willing to share. I believe we can meet our communities' needs by getting organized. One strategy comes through learning about the organizations that currently serve the communities, supporting them and expanding into areas they miss. I call my concept "Mensches in the Trenches," or Community Solutions for Community Problems. I currently have a Facebook page, Mensches In The Trenches, where I post information on people who are inspirational. Learning about caring people doing good in the community has moved me to tears at times. I hope you will take time and check it out. One of my favorite postings is about an amazing woman in Somaliland who took her passion for medicine, and ultimately created a hospital to serve the needs of women who would otherwise be neglected and die. Her name is Edna Adan, and she runs the Edna Adan Hospital in Somaliland. This woman is a Mensch!

People must be educated to abandon the culture of the selfish, "me first" mentality and join with an enlightened, altruistic approach to living with our fellow humans. We must rediscover the joy of giving. Many love and live the joy of giving briefly during the Christmas holidays. People dig into their pockets and share what they have cheerfully, and their hearts are happier for the experience. My saddest time of year is after New Year's Day, when things start to return to "normal," and people revert to selfishness.

I was fortunate to recover from drug and alcohol addiction in 1978, through a 12-step program. The 12th and final step asks us to show our gratitude for the gift of recovery we receive by helping others suffering from the affliction of addiction. We learn that there is a price for our gift of good health and happiness. It costs us the time and energy it takes to serve our fellow humans when we share the gift we are given.

Isn't life a gift? Don't we all have a debt of gratitude for the blessings we have in our lives? What better way to ensure that we appreciate our blessings than to keep ourselves aware of the debt we owe? What better way to enjoy the value in our lives than by recognizing the responsibility inherent in that debt? What better way to appreciate our gifts than to share with those less fortunate?

I have provided free massage at the wheelchair tennis tournament in Hilton Head, South Carolina, since the 1980s. Every time I show up with my equipment at the courts, my first thought as I look out and see the young men and women in their wheelchairs getting ready to play is, "And what do I have to complain about?" I become profoundly grateful that I am healthy and can walk unassisted. How often have I woken up in the morning and felt blessed that I could walk? The answer is, "Never!" But, without fail, when I arrive at this event, I am overwhelmed with a profound gratitude for my health. When I start massaging bodies that are covered in scars from years of surgeries associated with their accidents, as most of these players lost their ability to ambulate through car and motorcycle accidents, my heart aches for the years of pain they endured. I am never repelled by anything I see, and I'm always deeply moved by their courage and the humanity I experience. I'm inspired by them.

So many people live with a sense of spiritual emptiness that produces depression and inertia. They try to fill the hole in their soul with "things," as if they can satisfy the emptiness and feel happiness or satisfaction. They think that if they have enough possessions, they will be happy. Then, they feel their possessions possess them. They tell themselves if they are just pretty enough, or drunk enough, or rich enough, they will be happy. Then, one is stuck loving things and using people, instead of understanding our true nature, which is that we should love people and use things.

Only when we discover the true meaning and value of happiness, can we begin to experience the fruits of good living. People are so lost and lonely. Social media, Facebook included, can be a wonderful tool; however, too many people use it as a substitute for face-to-face interactions. There were times in my life when I felt very liked but so alone! Friendship through Facebook was without substance, like bubblegum is to nutrition—empty and deceptive in nature—all that chewing and no need to swallow. The warmth of human energy is vital to our spiritual wellbeing, and must be experienced "four eyes" (the Danish expression for meeting face to face).

The values that were alive in the sixties during the hippie culture were true and real. Even drugs, sex and rock 'n' roll started out as an innocent attempt to connect with each other. It was all about coming together (forgive the pun). Ultimately, I believe that drugs got us lost from the Utopia we were so close to finding. We knew that sharing was important, so we had crash pads where everyone was welcome to stay. We formed communes and pooled our resources, so that we could work and play together. We formed food co-operatives to increase our purchase power, so we could eat better. It is ironic to think that many people have finally made it to the communes of today, only they are now located in senior living facilities owned by corporations like Del Webb.

We brought a true innocence to everything we experienced. We were fresh and naive and hungry for the truth in our experiences. We were pure at heart, and we cared deeply about finding a path of righteousness. There was no Internet to bombard us with information. Our best time was spent with friends, making music, having adventures, and making love. Art was an important part of discovering our magic. Truly, we did not understand the magical phenomena of Woodstock until Joni Mitchell sang to us and helped us know how special we were. We were "stardust" and "golden," striving to return to the Garden of Eden, Mecca.

I identified myself as an experientialist. I believed that experiencing all of life was so very important. Trying something new and different was always valuable, because I grew in experience and wisdom. I didn't live my life vicariously the way people do today through television, video games, and the Internet. Life was real, and we were real. *"Make it art"* was a slogan that inspired my life to a higher plane

From all my experiences, the one that brought me most joy was the birth of my daughter, Lisa Ann Kasmir. In time, I would learn that the greatest gift parenting gave me was to teach me that I was not the center of the universe. That was reserved for my daughter's belly button.

Just learning that we are not the most important being is so valuable. Learning to put another person's needs ahead of our own is a huge growth step. I don't know how childless people learn this, but certainly raising my daughter was a lesson in valuing another above myself. I would like to believe that Lisa Ann is the best of me. I take great joy in watching her grow and mature into a kind, competent, generous being.

In my immediate future, I have a practical plan for bringing positive change to America. I will travel to colleges and high schools and lecture about the joys of giving. I want to teach young people how a democracy functions. Educating the young people in our communities is my top priority because I believe the importance of civics is lost on our younger citizens.

People need to understand that in a democracy, there is no such thing as not voting. In fact, when you do not vote, you just did. Often, the people who do not vote, in effect, cast their vote for the worst party by not voting for their opposition. This is the karma of voting.

Inaction is an action.

During my lectures, I will ask the volunteer organizations I have prearranged to take on recruits for a day to come onstage and describe their work. At the end of my program, I will invite people who are attending to volunteer for a day at the group of their choice, so they can experience the joy of giving firsthand. I believe that creating a pathway to giving will enable people who might not have volunteered the opportunity to enjoy the benefits of the experience. Making that first experience readily available reduces or eliminates the inertia, enabling people to overcome the huge obstacle of being left to their own devices to get started.

I have taken the best the sixties taught me and fashioned *The Hippie Manifesto*. It was there to inspire and guide me when I was in dire need of guidance. When my sister died, I was twelve and virtually abandoned by a family that could not cope with the loss. There I was, set adrift as I entered puberty. I desperately needed a set of values to guide me, and I don't know where I would be without those values. I never found this credo in any written form. I absorbed it through the music, my friendships, and the culture in general. It is a doctrine of goodness, natural living, and a commitment to harmony with Mother Earth.

I am now distilling it for you. I want it to be a guiding beacon that inspires you and all people to goodness

The Hippie Manifesto

>Love is the answer,
>Happiness, the key,
>Laughter, the tool.

Here are other thoughts you may find useful.
Life is a song you sing daily.
Live life in harmony with Mother Earth
Kindness is strength.
Fear is the absence of faith.
Sensitivity is essential.
We are all one family, and as such,
we are all in this together.
There is enough if we are willing to share.
Strength comes from unity
There is no "Away" as in "Throw it Away"
Everything is Here.
Everything is Now.
The love you take is equal to the love you make.
And finally,
It is never smart to be stupid.

All the joys of life await you if only you are willing to let go of old ideas and old habits. Selfishness must be the first to go! I promise you that the journey is worth it. If we live by these simple principles, together we will blossom. And peace will be more than a hope, a prayer, or a flower lifted by a young woman in a photograph.

"Come join us", Janrose said. "Throw down your guns and come over to our side!" Sadly, no takers. She was stonewalled.

Janrose Kasmir

Janrose cries out, "What are you going to do, shoot me?" This happened almost two years before Kent State.

FLOWER CHILD

Christian Zanani was so taken with the peaceful gesture Janrose embodied that he honored her photograph by recreating it in Legos.

Janrose Kasmir

In 2003 Janrose marched 8 KM on crutches in London protesting the impending War in Iraq, shortly after having knee surgery.

FLOWER CHILD

Janrose with photographer Marc Riboud in New York at a quiet moment. The most precious moments of her life were spent with Marc as he always believed in her as a peacemaker, reminding her of her place in history. He encouraged her to believe in herself as much as he did.

Janrose Kasmir

Made in the USA
Columbia, SC
01 May 2020